Wally,
The Fence Cat

Written by:
Donna Dobroski

Wally, The Fence Cat
Copyright © 2023 by Donna Dobroski

All rights reserved. No part of this publication may be reproduced, distributed, or transmitted in any form or by any means, including photocopying, recording, or other electronic or mechanical methods, without the prior written permission of the author, except in the case of brief quotations embodied in critical reviews and certain other non-commercial uses permitted by copyright law.

Tellwell Talent
www.tellwell.ca

ISBN
978-0-2288-5831-7 (Paperback)

Dedication:

This book is dedicated to all animal rescue groups, foster families, and volunteers who work tirelessly in assisting homeless, abandoned and needy animals throughout the world.

To all the people and organizations who donate financially and selflessly to animal welfare groups as well as those who open their hearts and homes to adopt pets.

One morning Nana looked
out her window.
She saw a big grey cat
sitting on her fence.
He sat there all day.

The next day he was there again.
She saw him walk along
the top of her fence.
He had very good balance.

Nana heard about a circus family.
They walked across a tight
rope in the circus.
Their name was the Wallenda family.
Nana decided to name the big
grey cat, Wally, because he was
like the Wallenda family.

Wally kept coming back.
Nana wondered if Wally was hungry.
She put some food on the
fence for Wally to eat.

Wally would not go to the
food while she was there.
Nana hid so Wally couldn't see her.
Wally came out and ate up all the food.

Day after day, Wally came
to Nana's fence.
He would never let Nana pet him.
When Nana tried, he would hiss, so
Nana hid where he couldn't see her.
Wally was afraid of people.

It was getting cold outside and Nana worried about Wally. Sometimes it rained on Wally. Sometimes it snowed on Wally. But Wally stayed on the fence and waited for Nana to feed him.

Nana heard about a lady named Beth.
Beth helped cats that
didn't have homes.
Nana called Beth and
asked for her help.

Beth gave Nana a special
cage to catch Wally.
Nana put food in the cage for Wally.
Wally went into the cage.
He ate the food and left the cage.

Nana put more food in the cage.
Wally ate the food and
left the cage, again.
Nana put more food in the cage.
This time she put it right at the back.
Wally went in and the door closed.
Wally was inside the cage.

Beth came and got Wally.
She took Wally to a vet.
A vet is an animal doctor.
The vet checked Wally all over.

Wally had some rotten teeth
that had to be fixed.
He got some needles so
he wouldn't get sick.
The vet took good care of Wally.

Afterwards, Wally stayed with Beth.
Beth really liked Wally but couldn't give him his forever home.
Nana couldn't give Wally his forever home, either.

Nana called Deanna.
Deanna loved to help animals.
She brought them to the vet when they were sick.
She made them feel safe.
Deanna found forever homes for animals, too.

Deanna called Susan.
Susan was sad because
she didn't have a cat.
Deanna told Susan about Wally.
Susan wanted Wally.
Susan adopted Wally.
Susan gave Wally his forever home.

Now Wally likes to be petted.
He likes to snuggle in Susan's lap.
Wally doesn't hiss anymore.
He purrs.
Susan likes to hear Wally purr.

Wally has a good home.
Susan loves Wally.
Wally loves Susan.
Wally loves his forever home.

Wally is happy.
Susan is happy.
Beth is happy.
Deanna is happy.
And Nana is happy too.

Acknowledgement:

Deanna Maerz, founder of "Angel Animal Rescue" aka AARF

Beth Koruna, "Hamilton Community Cat Network"

Susan Skritich, Wally's new "mother"

Amanda and Myles Faulkner, who took care of Wally prior to "Nana" and who along with their family and other generous donors who contributed financially to AARF for Wally's medical expenses.

www.ingramcontent.com/pod-product-compliance
Lightning Source LLC
LaVergne TN
LVHW070047070526
838200LV00028B/414